W9-BAG-183

READ ABOUT

Birds

Jen Green

COPPER BEECH BOOKS

BROOKFIELD • CONNECTICUT

Contents

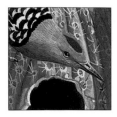

1 What Are Birds?   **page 3**

Feathers • Eggs • Where Do Birds Live? • Bodies

2 Feathers and Flying   **page 10**

Wings • Gliding • Hovering • Migration

3 Birds That Don't Fly   **page 15**

Birds That Swim • Runners • No Enemies!

4 What Do Birds Eat?   **page 17**

Meat- and Plant-Eaters • Beaks • Hunting

5 Living Together   **page 22**

Flocks • Birdsong • Finding a Mate

6 A Bird's Life   **page 26**

Nests • Eggs • Chicks • Growing Up • Age

Find Out More   **page 30**

Index and Picture Answers   **page 32**

MA EM FM AH LMc HHA.

© Aladdin Books Ltd 2000

Designed and produced by
Aladdin Books Ltd
28 Percy Street
London W1P 0LD

First published in
the United States in 2000 by
Copper Beech Books,
an imprint of
The Millbrook Press,
2 Old New Milford Road
Brookfield, Connecticut 06804

ISBN 0-7613-1216-1
Cataloging-in-Publication data is on file
at the Library of Congress.

Printed in U.A.E.

Editor
Jim Pipe

Science Consultant
David Burnie

Series Literacy Consultant
Wendy Cobb

Design
Flick, Book Design and Graphics

Picture Research
Brooks Krikler Research

What Are Birds?

Feathers • Eggs • Where Do Birds Live? • Bodies

Birds are all around you, whether you live in a crowded city or on an island in the middle of the ocean.

Like us, birds breathe air and have warm bodies. Unlike us, birds have feathers all over their bodies. Feathers keep a bird's body warm and dry, and help them to fly.

A roadrunner can't fly fast, but it is very quick on its feet.

All birds have wings, and most birds can soar and swoop through the air. Their feathery tails help them to balance in the air and also on the ground. Some birds are good swimmers.

Most birds have bare, scaly legs without feathers. Instead of jaws with teeth, birds have a tough, horny beak.

Kingfishers are strong flyers. Like many birds, they also find food underwater.

Birds don't give birth to babies, as people do. Instead, their babies grow inside eggs with hard shells. When they start a family, most birds make a nest and lay their eggs there.

When the babies hatch out, the parent birds feed and care for them until they are old enough to look after themselves.

Birds don't make nests to sleep in. They build nests to make a safe place for their eggs and young.

Beak catches fish.

Feathers keep body warm and dry.

Clawed feet grab branch.

This parrot is one of many colorful birds that live in the rain forest.

Birds live almost everywhere on Earth. They are found in leafy woods and hot, dusty deserts, on windy cliffs and snowy mountains.

Many penguins live in icy places.

Birds live in the far north and south of our planet, where the weather is always cold and icy. Many birds spend all their lives by seas, lakes, or rivers, and some can dive deep underwater.

How many different birds can you name? Scientists have discovered over 9,000 different types, or species (say "spee-shees") of birds.

Gila woodpeckers live in the deserts of Central America. They make nests by pecking holes in cactus plants.

Most birds are made for flying. With their thin shape, they slip easily through the air. Inside their bodies, birds have a skeleton. But their bones are very light to help them fly.

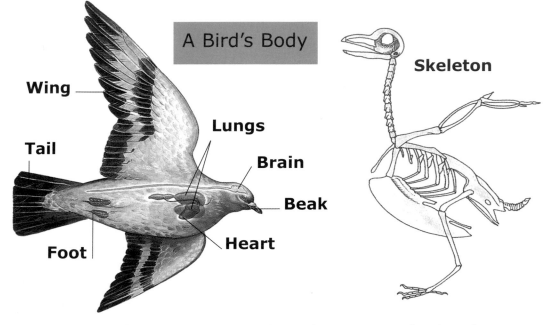

A Bird's Body

Wing

Tail

Foot

Lungs

Brain

Heart

Beak

Skeleton

Birds see and hear well. They use their sharp senses to find food. Under their skin, birds have some of the same body parts that we do.

Birds have a heart to pump blood around the body, lungs so they can breathe, and muscles so they can move. They have two stomachs to help them break down their food.

All birds have the same body parts, with two legs, two wings, a beak, and a tail, but they can look very different.

Some birds have very long necks and thin legs. Other birds are short and chunky. Each bird's shape helps it move about and find its food.

Many eagles and hawks use their sharp, hooked claws to catch fish, mice, rabbits, or small birds.

Ducks' bodies are shaped like boats. Their webbed feet work like paddles.

To grab onto branches, many small birds' feet have three toes in front, and one behind.

9

Feathers and Flying

Wings • Gliding • Hovering • Migration

Birds have three different kinds of feathers. Body feathers cover most of the bird's body and protect it. Fluffy down feathers next to the bird's skin keep it warm. Long flight feathers on the wings and tail help birds to fly.

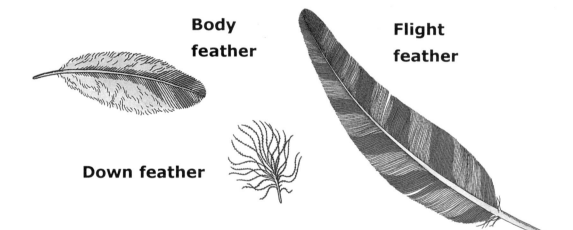

Body feather

Flight feather

Down feather

Birds take great care of their feathers. They comb them with their beaks to clean off dirt and insects. This is called preening.

At least once a year, the old, worn-out feathers drop out, and fresh, new feathers grow in their place.

What is this bird doing? Answer on page 32.

Waxwings

Many birds have gray, brown, or streaked feathers. These colors help birds to hide from their enemies.

Other birds have bright feathers which help them to find a mate (see page 24).

Flamingo feathers turn pink because of the pink shellfish the birds eat.

Flying helps birds to find food and escape from enemies such as cats.

Birds' wings have a special curved shape like an airplane wing. When the air rushes past this shape, it lifts them up into the air.

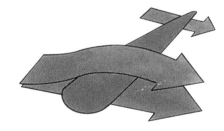

Birds' wings are round on top and flat below.

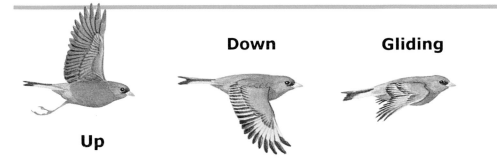

Up

Down

Gliding

Birds move forward by flapping their wings. As the wings flap up, many feathers part to let the air through, and the wings partly fold in next to the body. As the wings flap down, the feathers close to push against the air.

Different kinds of birds fly in different ways. Albatrosses and boobies hold their strong wings out stiffly to glide on the wind.

This blue-footed booby is good at gliding.

Kestrel

Kestrels can hover like helicopters. They beat their wings very quickly to stay in one place in the air.

Some birds use their flying skills to go on long journeys, called migrations. Each year, they make a round trip of thousands of miles.

In the spring, these birds fly to where there is plenty of food to raise a family. In the fall, they fly back again to escape the winter cold.

These geese are migrating.

Birds That Don't Fly

Birds That Swim • Runners • No Enemies!

Some birds can't fly at all. Instead, they are mainly very good at swimming or running, so they can escape from enemies and catch food.

Many penguins live in the Antarctic in the far south of our planet. Their wings are shaped like flippers. Underwater, they flap their wings to "fly" through the sea.

Penguins are good swimmers.

Ostriches are very fast runners. In grasslands and deserts, they can race along at over forty mph. Their feet have two broad toes which spread out to stop them from sinking into the sand.

The speedy ostrich

Some birds that live on islands stopped flying because there were no animals around that hunted them — until people came along!

The cormorant (left) from the Galapagos Islands and the kakapo from New Zealand stopped flying because they had no enemies.

What Do Birds Eat?

Birds eat many different kinds of foods. Finches, pigeons, and parrots eat mainly plant food, including seeds, nuts, fruit, and buds.

Swallows and woodpeckers hunt insects. Blackbirds and thrushes eat juicy worms and snails. Pelicans and herons catch fish in seas and rivers. Vultures feed on dead animals.

How does this heron catch slippery fish? The answer is on page 32.

Some birds eat only one type of food. Others eat many different foods. Crows and gulls eat anything they can find.

Birds use their beaks to catch and eat their food. Beaks come in different shapes and sizes. The shape of a bird's beak can help you guess the type of food it eats.

Little hummingbirds feed on nectar, a sugary liquid found in flowers. With their long, thin beaks and tongues, they can reach right inside bell-shaped flowers to drink.

Hummingbirds beat their wings very fast so they can hover near a flower while they drink its nectar.

Pelicans dive into the sea, using their pouch like a fishing net.

Avocets live on muddy seashores. As an avocet walks across the mud, it swishes its long, thin beak from side to side to find worms and shellfish.

Avocet

Ducks feed on tiny plants and animals that live in ponds or seas. Their flat beaks work like sieves as they strain food from the water.

Black-headed gull

Vulture

Not all birds catch their food. Vultures and ravens eat the bodies of dead animals. Gulls are like pirates – they often steal food from other birds.

Many eagles and hawks feed on mice, rabbits, or small birds, which they catch with their sharp claws. Their hooked beaks tear their meat into pieces small enough to swallow.

Most birds find their food by day, but owls hunt as night falls. Their large eyes can see well in low light. With their sharp ears, they can hear the tiny sounds mice make as they scurry along.

This owl's fluffy feathers make very little noise when it flies.

Living Together

Flocks • Birdsong • Finding a Mate

Some kinds of birds live in pairs or on their own, except when it is time to mate and raise a family. Other birds spend their whole lives in a group called a flock.

A flock of plovers looking for a place to sleep.

Starlings live and feed in noisy flocks. As each bird pecks at seeds on the ground, it checks for danger. If it sees an enemy, it gives a cry, and the whole group takes off at once.

Every type of bird has its own call, or song.

Birds use their voices to keep the group together. If a flock of geese flies overhead, you will hear them honk to keep in touch.

Some birds can only croak or squawk. Other birds can sing a song — a long stream of twitters and trills. Parent birds can recognize their chicks by their voices. Male and female birds also have different voices.

Some birds keep the same partner for life. Others choose a new mate every year. It's usually the males that try to win the females.

Many male birds have beautiful feathers. The females pick the most handsome to mate with.

Nightingales have very dull feathers, but they sing beautifully. In spring, the male birds sing long and loud to win a partner. Their songs also tell rival males to keep away.

What's this bird doing? Answer on page 32.

Japanese cranes dance to win their mates.

Male terns feed the females to get them to mate with them.

Terns

Japanese cranes

To impress the females, some male birds of paradise hang upside down from tree branches and spread out their long tails.

A male bird of paradise shows off its feathers.

A Bird's Life

Nests • Eggs • Chicks • Growing Up • Age

Birds build nests as warm, safe places to lay their eggs and bring up their babies. They use the materials they find around them to build with. Twigs, leaves, grass, moss, and mud are all used to make nests.

Goldcrest nest

Some birds line the inside of their nest with soft wool or feathers.

Razorbill nest

Woodpeckers drill out nest holes in old, soft tree trunks with their strong beaks. Razorbills nest on ledges or between rocks, and puffins dig burrows in sandy cliffs.

Eggs look different on the outside.

But inside all chicks grow in the same way.

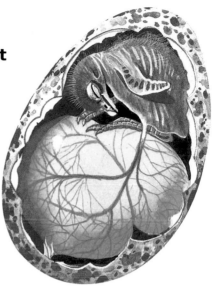

When the nest is ready, the female lays her eggs there. She sits on the eggs to keep them warm while the chicks grow inside. After a while, the eggs are ready. The baby birds peck a hole in the shell and push their way out.

Ringed plovers lay their eggs on beaches. Their eggs look just like pebbles!

Young blackbirds open wide for a juicy worm.

Ducklings and other chicks that hatch out in nests on the ground are stronger than baby birds that hatch in nests in trees, such as young blackbirds.

Ducklings are born with a covering of fluffy feathers. Their eyes open quickly, and they are soon strong enough to stand, walk, and swim. Newborn blackbirds have no fluffy feathers to protect them. They cannot see or stand, or feed themselves. For a few weeks, their parents bring them grubs and worms to eat.

The young birds grow fast, and their feathers sprout. They can fly without being taught, but need months of practice to become skillful flyers.

Young birds leave their parents when they are a few weeks old. Some join a flock, others live alone until they are old enough to mate.

Most adult birds have a new family once or twice a year for as long as they live — which can be as long as eighty years.

Condors have lived for over seventy-five years in zoos, but few will live this long in the wild.

Find Out More

PICTURE QUIZ

Can you remember the names of the birds below? Which of them can fly? If you need some help, turn to pages 3, 4, 7, 9, 16, and 21. The answers are on page 32.

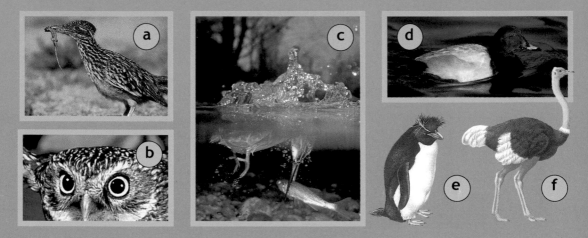

a

b

c

d

e

f

UNUSUAL WORDS

Here we explain some words you may have read in this book.

Bill Another word for a bird's beak.

Down Soft, fluffy feathers that lie next to a bird's skin and help it to keep warm.

Flock A large group of birds that live, feed, and fly together.

Hatch When a baby bird breaks out of its egg.

Egg

Migrations Regular journeys that animals make each year to find food, raise a family, or avoid the cold of winter.

Nectar A sweet, sugary liquid made by plants.

Preening When a bird nibbles at its feathers with its beak to clean off dirt and remove insects.

Song A series of different notes made by a bird to send messages to other birds.

Species A particular kind of animal or plant.

RECORD BREAKERS
Biggest and Smallest Birds
The ostrich stands eight feet high. Its eggs are bigger than grapefruits! The bee hummingbird is only two inches long from beak to tail-tip.

Fastest Bird
Peregrine falcons are the fastest flyers. They can dive through the air at speeds of up to 180 mph.

THE ANIMAL KINGDOM
Scientists have put animals into groups to show how they are related. Birds are closest to mammals and reptiles.

ANIMALS WITH BACKBONES

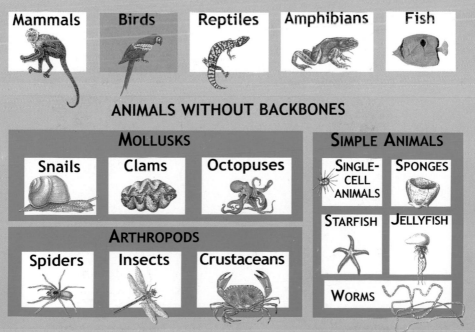

Mammals   Birds   Reptiles   Amphibians   Fish

ANIMALS WITHOUT BACKBONES

MOLLUSKS
Snails   Clams   Octopuses

ARTHROPODS
Spiders   Insects   Crustaceans

SIMPLE ANIMALS
SINGLE-CELL ANIMALS   SPONGES
STARFISH   JELLYFISH
WORMS

Index

Albatrosses 13
Avocets 20

Beaks 4, 5, 18, 20, 21, 26, 30, 31
Bills 30
Birds of paradise 25
Blackbirds 17, 28
Boobies 13

Chicks 23, 27, 28
Condors 29
Cormorants 16
Cranes 25
Crows 18

Down 10, 30
Ducks 9, 20, 28, 32

Eagles 9, 21
Eggs 5, 26, 27, 31

Falcons 31
Feathers 3, 5, 10, 11, 12, 21, 24, 28, 29, 30
Finches 17
Flamingoes 12

Flocks 22, 23, 29, 30
Flying 3, 4, 8, 12-13, 29, 30, 31
Food 17-21, 28

Geese 14, 23
Goldcrest 26
Gulls 18, 20

Hatching 5, 27, 28, 30
Hawks 9, 21
Herons 17, 32
Hummingbirds 18, 31

Kakapos 16
Kestrels 14
Kingfishers 4, 32

Mates 24, 25
Migration 14, 30

Nectar 18, 30
Nests 5, 26, 27
Nightingales 24

Ostriches 16, 31, 32
Owls 21, 32

Parrots 6, 17
Peacocks 32
Pelicans 17, 19
Penguins 7, 15, 32
Plovers 22, 27
Preening 10, 30
Puffins 26

Ravens 20
Razorbills 26
Roadrunners 3, 32

Senses 8
Shelducks 11, 32
Songs 23, 24, 30
Species 7, 30
Starlings 22
Swallows 17
Swimming 4, 15, 28

Terns 25
Thrushes 17

Vultures 17, 20

Woodpeckers 7, 17, 26

ANSWERS TO PICTURE QUESTIONS

Page 11 The bird, a shelduck, is cleaning its feathers by nibbling at them.

Page 17 The heron has long, thin legs for wading through the water and a long, sharp beak which it uses to spear fish.

Page 24 Peacocks show off to females with a fan of feathers.

Page 31 a is a roadrunner, b is an owl, c is a kingfisher, d is a duck, e is a penguin, and f is an ostrich. All of them fly, apart from the penguin and the ostrich.

Photocredits: Abbreviations: t-top, m-middle, b-bottom, r-right, l-left, c-center.
Cover & pages—9bl & br, 13, 14, 22, 23, 28, 29, 30tr & 31—Stockbyte. 1, 6, 9m, 12 & 24—Digital Stock.
3, 4, 11, 21, 30tl, tm & ml—Bruce Coleman Collection. 19—Oxford Scientific Films.
Illustrators: Joanne Cowne, Chris Shields, Justine Peek, Dave Burroughs, John Rignall.